A Three-Year Course in Junior Cycle

LOUDER THAN WORDS

ALY ALLSOPP
SEANAGH McCARTHY
CIARA MORRIS

GRAMMAR GUIDE

educate.ie

educate.ie

PUBLISHED BY:
Educate.ie

Walsh Educational Books Ltd
Castleisland, Co. Kerry, Ireland

www.educate.ie

EDITOR:
Caitriona Clarke

DESIGN:
Liz White Designs

LAYOUT:
Jen Patton

PRINTED AND BOUND BY:
Walsh Colour Print, Castleisland

© Aly Allsopp, Seanagh McCarthy, Ciara Morris, 2022

Without limiting the rights under copyright, this book is sold subject to the condition that it shall not, by way of trade or otherwise, be reproduced, stored in or introduced into a retrieval system, or transmitted, in any form or by any means (electronic, mechanical, photocopying, recording or otherwise), or otherwise circulated, without the publisher's prior consent, in any form other than that in which it is published and without a similar condition, including this condition, being imposed on the subsequent publisher. The author and publisher have made every effort to trace all copyright holders, but if some have been inadvertently overlooked, we would be happy to make the necessary arrangements at the first opportunity.

ISBN: 978-1-914586-41-5

COPYRIGHT PERMISSIONS:
Shutterstock

Contents

Introduction iv

Nouns 1
Pronouns 4
Verbs 8
Tenses 11
Adjectives 16
Adverbs 20
Prepositions 24
Conjunctions 27
Capital letters 32
Full stops 37
Commas 41
Question marks 45
Exclamation marks 49
Apostrophes 52
Quotation marks 56
Synonyms 60
Antonyms 63
Superlatives 65
Homophones 68

Common clangers 72

Grammar at a Glance 75

Introduction

The English language has changed over time but, like every language, there are rules for writing, spelling and punctuation.

- Being able to identify these rules will help you to respond to questions about Junior Cycle English texts more effectively.
- Being able to apply these rules to your own writing will allow you to communicate more clearly and creatively.

Each grammar point in this guide is organised using the acronym **GRAMMAR**, as follows:

Get to grips with …	An introduction to the grammar point, part of speech, punctuation lesson, etc.
Read the examples	Examples of the grammar point in action
Attempt it yourself	A short exercise to get you started
More practice	More opportunities to practise using the grammar point
More practice	Further opportunities to perfect your writing using the grammar point
Another fact	More useful or interesting information about the grammar point
Retrieval exercise	The chance to go back over what you learned and check in to see what you remember

📷 *For the gram*

This feature offers tips for using grammar correctly and avoiding common mistakes.

NOUNS

Get to grips with ... nouns

A noun is a person, animal, place or thing.

Read the examples

Person	Animal	Place	Thing
boy	pig	Paris	chair
child	dog	Ireland	book
Derek	cat	Limerick	phone
student	shark	Letterkenny	cheese
grandmother	elephant	Europe	road

Attempt it yourself

Turn the noun around

1. **(a)** Unscramble the letters to find the nouns.

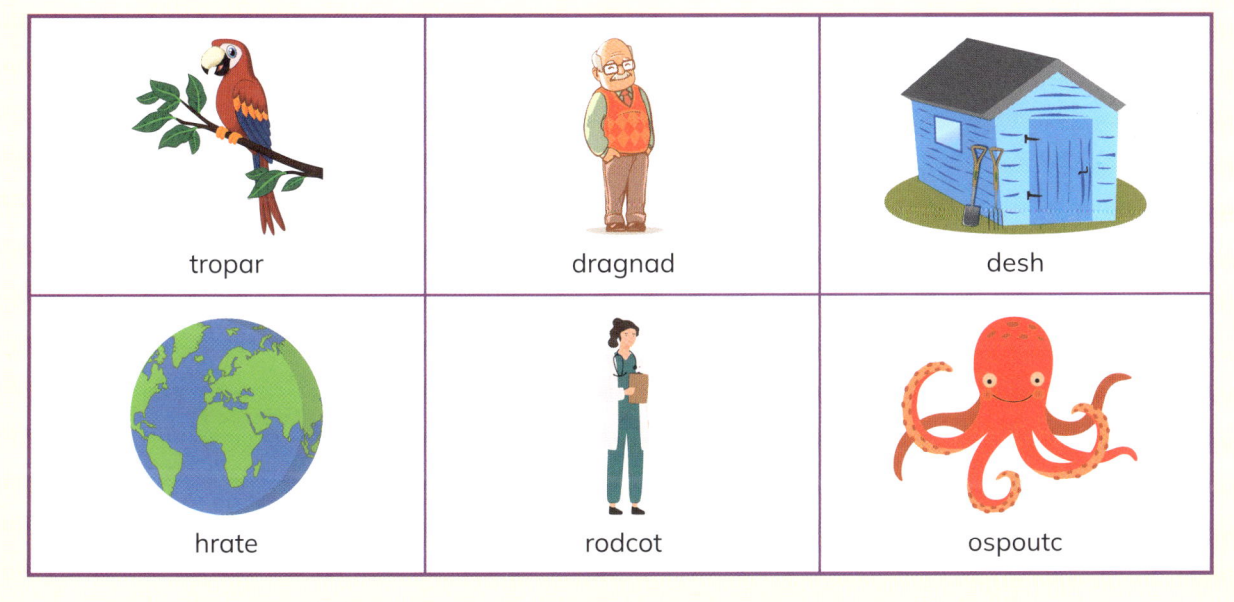

tropar	dragnad	desh
hrate	rodcot	ospoutc

1

(b) Now sort the nouns by writing them into the correct category in the table below.

Person	Animal	Place	Thing

More practice

Noun detective

2. Open any page of your English textbook, novel or school journal. Make a list of all the nouns you can find on that page.

More practice

Noun finder

3. Circle the nouns.

nurse	and	Berlin	bird	hairdresser	mine	door
bike	the	lamp	Wicklow	us	monkey	there

4. Underline the nouns in the following excerpt from *Matilda* by Roald Dahl.

> From then on, Matilda would visit the library only once a week in order to take out new books and return the old ones. Her own small bedroom now became her reading-room and there she would sit and read most afternoons, often with a mug of hot chocolate beside her. She was not quite tall enough to reach things around the kitchen, but she kept a small box in the outhouse which she brought in and stood on in order to get whatever she wanted. Mostly it was hot chocolate she made, warming the milk in a saucepan on the stove before mixing it. Occasionally she made Bovril or Ovaltine. It was pleasant to take a hot drink up to her room and have it beside her as she sat in her silent room reading in the empty house in the afternoons. The books transported her into new worlds and introduced her to amazing people who lived exciting lives. She went on olden-day sailing ships with Joseph Conrad. She went to Africa with Ernest Hemingway and to India with Rudyard Kipling. She travelled all over the world while sitting in her little room in an English village.

Another fact

Examine the following sentence from *The Burning* by Laura Bates.

[place] [people]

In a small **playground**, three **girls** who are really too big for it are whizzing around on the **roundabout**.

[thing]

Retrieval exercise

In your own words, write down what a noun is. Include an example to help you revise.

A noun is ....
....
An example of a noun (person) is: ....
An example of a noun (animal) is: ....
An example of a noun (place) is: ....
An example of a noun (thing) is: ....

Louder than Words >> Grammar Guide

PRONOUNS

Get to grips with ... pronouns

Pronouns are words that are used instead of nouns. Remember that a noun is a person, animal, place or thing.

Pronoun list

I	me	we	us	you	he
him	she	her	it	they	them
my	mine	your	yours	his	hers
its	our	ours	their	theirs	itself
myself	yourself	herself	himself	ourselves	themselves

- Personal pronouns are used in place of a noun when the noun is a person or thing.

   Examples
   it, she, I, you, him, we

- Possessive pronouns show ownership.

   Examples
   my, her, his, their, our, yours

- Preferred pronouns: Some people prefer to be referred to as they/them. Therefore, they/them can be used to refer to one person as well as to a group of people.

Read the examples

Patrycja walked the dog before Patrycja went to see Patrycja's cousins.	→	Patrycja walked the dog before **she** went to see **her** cousins.
Femi went for a run before Femi had to catch Femi's bus to school.	→	Femi went for a run before **he** had to catch **his** bus to school.
Can Jack, Elijah and Lucas come to my party?	→	Can **they** come to my party?
The students grabbed the students' coats and put the coats on.	→	They grabbed **their** coats and put **them** on.
Grace passed Grace's driving test and said the driving test was easy.	→	**She** passed **her** driving test and said **it** was easy.
Ben has informed Ben's teachers that Ben's preferred pronouns are they/them.	→	**They** have informed **their** teachers that **their** preferred pronouns are they/them.

Pronouns

Attempt it yourself

Provide the pronoun

1. Circle the pronouns.

her	they	ahead	it	fast	them	and
you	mine	the	his	yours	us	this	does

2. Rewrite the following sentences by replacing the underlined words with suitable pronouns.

   (a) Sam jumped out from behind a tree so Sam could scare his little sister.

   ....
   ....
   ....

   (b) Ryan, Daniel and David are going to Portugal at Easter and Ryan, Daniel and David can't wait.

   ....
   ....
   ....

   (c) Melanie picked up the ball and threw the ball to her friend.

   ....
   ....
   ....

   (d) Stella and Simone are twins and sometimes people get Stella and Simone mixed up.

   ....
   ....
   ....

   (e) Ronan made a hot chocolate for Ronan.

   ....
   ....
   ....

More practice

Pronoun detective

3. Open any page of your English textbook, novel or school journal. Make a list of all the pronouns you can find on that page.

....
....
....
....
....
....
....
....
....
....
....
....

More practice

Perfect pronouns

4. Underline the pronouns in the following excerpt from *George's Marvellous Medicine* by Roald Dahl.

'I know a great many secrets,' she said, and suddenly she smiled. It was a thin icy smile, the kind a snake might make just before it bites you. 'Come over here to Grandma and she'll whisper secrets to you.'

5. Choose a pronoun from the list below to complete the following sentences.

| we | their | my | them | I | you |

(a) I walk _____ dog every day after school.

(b) My uncle came to visit us but _____ were out.

(c) Did _____ see who rang the doorbell?

(d) My friend had to explain the game because _____ didn't know how to play.

(e) The teacher asked the students if he could help _____ with _____ homework.

Pronouns

Pronoun poetry

6. Complete the stanza by adding pronouns. Add a title to the poem and write one more stanza.

Title: _____

First stanza:

_____ said to _____

Why can't _____ see

The fun in store

For _____ and _____

Second stanza:

....
....
....
....
....

Another fact

Examine the following sentence from *King and the Dragonflies* by Kacen Callender.

He shrugs, like **he** can hear all **my** questions and **he** doesn't know any of the answers **himself**.

Retrieval exercise

In your own words, write down what a pronoun is. Include an example to help you revise.

A pronoun is ....
....
....
....

What are your pronouns?

She/her ☐

He/him ☐

They/them ☐

VERBS

Get to grips with ... verbs

Verbs are action (or doing) words. They are used to describe an action, state or occurrence. Every sentence needs a verb.

Read the examples

John **climbed** the stairs.
The dog **chased** the cat.
Cara **plays** the guitar.

Attempt it yourself

Verb finder

1. (a) Circle the verbs in each list.

(i)	sing	high	speak	think	sweet	sting	grab
(ii)	play	print	read	sweaty	fantastic	mask	thought
(iii)	jump	sleepy	rest	practise	impact	stuff	forgetful

(b) Can you find any words in the above lists that are nouns as well as verbs? List them here.

....
....
....
....

More practice

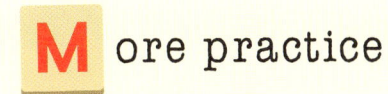

Action art

2. Write out as many verbs as you can for the following images.

(a)

(b)

(c)

(d)

(e)

📷 For the gram

Try to vary the verbs you use in your own writing. For example, instead of saying 'He **walked** along the road, **carrying** his heavy bag and **saying** …' try 'He **trudged** along the road, **dragging** his heavy bag and **muttering** …'

You can use a thesaurus to find **synonyms** of verbs (see page 60).

More practice

Verbs and verses

3. Write out ten lines from your favourite song. Underline all the verbs you can find.

Louder than Words >> Grammar Guide

Verb me

4. Come up with a verb for each letter in your name.

> **Example**
> Ciara: **C**atch **I**nsist **A**dvance **R**emain **A**sk

....

....

Another fact

When **auxiliary verbs** are added to a sentence, they change the tense of the verb that follows.

- Auxiliary verbs 'shall' and 'will' make the sentence future tense.

> **Examples**
> I **shall** go to the shops.   He **will** fight back.

- Auxiliary verbs 'could', 'should' and 'would' make the sentence conditional tense.

> **Examples**
> I **could** play tennis if I had better upper body strength.
> He **should** study for his exams.
> She **would** love to go to the play but she doesn't have a babysitter.

📷 For the gram

When you combine 'could', 'should' or 'would' with 'have', you can use the contractions 'could've', 'should've' or 'would've', e.g. 'I **should've** gone to the shops but I left it too late'.

Remember that these contractions do not stand for 'could of', 'should of' or 'would of' – this is a common mistake as they sound similar when said out loud. However, they are always incorrect.

Retrieval exercise

In your own words, write down what a verb is. Include an example to help you revise.

A verb is ....

....

An example of a verb: ....

10

TENSES

Get to grips with ... tenses

The meaning of a verb can be changed by changing the tense. The tense shows whether the action is taking place in the past, present or future.

- The present tense describes things that are happening right now, in the present moment. The present tense also describes things that happen on a regular basis.
- The past tense describes things that have already happened. It is a finished action in the past.
- The future tense describes things that will happen in the future.

For the gram

It is important to identify and stick to the tense in which you are writing. A common mistake is to jump between different tenses. When you are telling a story, decide whether your narrator is describing events as they are happening (present tense), looking back on events that have already taken place (past tense) or imagining events that might take place (future tense).

Read the examples

Here are some verbs in the past, present and future tenses.

Verb	Past tense	Present tense	Future tense
Do	I did I have done	I do I am doing	I will do
See	I saw I have seen	I see I am seeing	I will see
Write	I wrote I have written	I write I am writing	I will write
Teach	I taught I have taught	I teach I am teaching	I will teach
Bring	I brought I have brought	I bring I am bringing	I will bring

Louder than Words >> Grammar Guide

Attempt it yourself

Tense times

1. Rewrite the following text from books and films in a different tense, e.g. from past to present.

   Examples
   George lived in a small town where everyone was obsessed with Spice Bags.
   George lives in a small town where everyone is obsessed with Spice Bags.
   (From *Mr Spicebag* by Freddie Alexander)

   (a) Mr. and Mrs. Dursley of number four, Privet Drive, were proud to say that they were perfectly normal, thank you very much.
   (From *Harry Potter and the Philosopher's Stone* by J.K. Rowling)

   ....
   ....

   (b) Simon leans forward with his elbows on the desk, looking spring-loaded and ready to pounce on fresh gossip. (From *One of Us Is Lying* by Karen M. McManus)

   ....
   ....

   (c) This world is rotten, and those who are making it rot deserve to die.
   (From *Death Note* by Tsugumi Ohba)

   ....
   ....

   (d) All those moments will be lost in time, like tears in rain. (From the film *Blade Runner*)

   ....
   ....

(e) Late in the winter of my seventeenth year, my mother decided I was depressed, presumably because I never left the house, spent quite a lot of time in bed, read the same book over and over, ate infrequently, and devoted quite a bit of my abundant free time to thinking about death.

(From *The Fault in Our Stars* by John Green)

More practice

Tense sense

2. (a) Use a tick ✓ or an ✗ to indicate whether the past tense has been used correctly or incorrectly in the following sentences.

   (i) Maria did an excellent CBA presentation all about sailing. ☐

   (ii) Julie brings all her books home from school. ☐

   (iii) When I get to school, I tidy my locker. ☐

   (iv) Yesterday I was so tired, I was in bed by 8 p.m.! ☐

   (v) Steven chooses a film for their family to watch. ☐

   (vi) I wouldn't go to school if I am sick. ☐

   (vii) Ahmed found his football boots under the bed. ☐

   (viii) Lucia read her book and looks out of the window. ☐

(b) Rewrite the incorrect sentences using the past tense.

Louder than Words >> Grammar Guide

More practice

Tense sense

3. **(a)** Use a tick ✓ or an ✗ to indicate whether the present tense has been used correctly or incorrectly in the following sentences.

   (i) Fiona ran to meet Joseph. ☐

   (ii) I was studying at my granny's house. ☐

   (iii) Thomas writes with his left hand. ☐

   (iv) My sister drinks tea every morning. ☐

   (v) Jennifer will try to come to the party. ☐

   (b) Rewrite the incorrect sentences using the present tense.

Another fact

When you're telling a story, make sure to be consistent with your tenses. Read the following passage written in the past tense.

Rosie dragged herself out of bed and listened to the rain banging on the windows. She couldn't believe her match was going ahead, even with a yellow weather warning in place. Sometimes her coach was just plain reckless. 'Oh well,' she sighed, pulling her boots and kit out of the cupboard, noticing the dried mud from last week's match still lingering.

(a) Underline all the verbs in the past tense.

(b) Rewrite the passage in the present tense.

Rewrite the following passage, making the tenses consistent.

Just when she thought it was safe to come out, she hears a sound from the hallway. She slides out from under the bed and listened intently. Who are these men? What will they want? Her mind raced as she is trying to find her phone. She will call her neighbour, she thinks to herself.

Retrieval exercise

In your own words, write down what tense is. Include examples to help you revise.

Tense is

An example of a verb in the past tense:

An example of a verb in the present tense:

An example of a verb in the future tense:

ADJECTIVES

Get to grips with ... adjectives

Adjectives are words that are used to describe nouns or pronouns. They help to describe something in more detail. Their use will make your writing easier for your reader to picture and imagine.

Read the examples

blue car	**super** song	**yellow** sun	**grey** day
big dog	**great** film	**green** grass	**difficult** exam
silly uncle	**busy** road	**dark** sky	**easy** homework

Attempt it yourself

Adjective alliteration

1. Come up with two alliterative adjectives for the following nouns.

Examples
fluffy frolicking sheep

(a) _____ _____ cup
(b) _____ _____ phone
(c) _____ _____ sister
(d) _____ _____ table
(e) _____ _____ pen
(f) _____ _____ dog
(g) _____ _____ chair
(h) _____ _____ street
(i) _____ _____ bus

Adjectives

More practice

Clap the adjectives

2. Working on your own or as a class, read the following passage aloud. Clap every time you hear an adjective.

> The young girl ran quickly across the grey road. When she reached the other side, she noticed the green grass was mucky underfoot. Checking to make sure her trendy, white runners were not dirty, she walked briskly to the sliding doors of the large supermarket. The aisles were wide and bright and filled with delicious sweets. She tapped her pocket to ensure her big, shiny euro coin was still there. Choosing sour, yellow sweets and tasty white chocolate buttons, she went to the high counter to pay the grumpy cashier and then skipped happily home.

Adjective sense

3. See how many adjectives you can come up with in three minutes for the five senses.

Touch	Taste	Smell	Sight	Sound
......	......	......	......	......
......	......	......	......	......
......	......	......	......	......
......	......	......	......	......
......	......	......	......	......

Say what you see

4. Describe the scene below using as many adjectives as possible.

Louder than Words >> Grammar Guide

Blocked adjective challenge

5. Write a description of the following characters *without* using the three adjectives given under their images.

(a)

old   grey   frail

(b)

young   blond   sporty

(c)

happy   curly   professional

More practice
Adjective finder

6. Underline the adjectives in the following excerpt from *Harry Potter and the Philosopher's Stone* by J.K. Rowling.

> And the fleet of little boats moved off all at once, gliding across the lake, which was as smooth as glass. Everyone was silent, staring up at the great castle overhead. It towered over them as they sailed nearer and nearer to the cliff on which it stood.
>
> 'Heads down!' yelled Hagrid as the first boat reached the cliff; they all bent their heads and the little boats carried them through a curtain of ivy which hid a wide opening in the cliff face. They were carried along a dark tunnel, which seemed to be taking them right underneath the castle, until they reached a kind of underground harbour, where they clambered out on to the rocks and pebbles.

7. Underline the adjectives in the following excerpt from *Great Expectations* by Charles Dickens.

> She was dressed in rich materials – satins, and lace and silks – all of white. Her shoes were white. And she had a long white veil dependent from her hair, and she had bridal flowers in her hair, and her hair was white. Some bright jewels sparkled on her neck and on her hands, and some other jewels lay sparkling on the table. Dresses, less splendid than the dress she wore, and half packed trunks, were scattered about.

Another fact

Examine the following sentence.

> The **great**, **green** grasshopper leaped over the **pretty**, **colourful** flowers.

Retrieval exercise

In your own words, write down what an adjective is. Include an example to help you revise.

An adjective is ....
....
....
....
....

An example of an adjective: ....

ADVERBS

Get to grips with ... adverbs

Adverbs are used to describe verbs in more detail. They add more description and detail to sentences. Their use will improve your writing as they will create a piece that is more *skilfully* and *beautifully* constructed.

Adverbs usually end in -ly; however, this is **not always** the case. For example, the following words are adverbs but do not end in -ly:

| fast | never | better | often | almost |

- Adverbs of manner tell us how an action occurs:

    He ran **quickly**.

- Adverbs of place tell us where an action occurs:

    Come **here**.

- Adverbs of time tell us when an action occurs:

    Let's go **tomorrow**.

- Adverbs of frequency tell us how often an action occurs:

    I **frequently** walk to school.

- Adverbs of degree tell us about the intensity or degree of something:

    They were **extremely** angry.

- Interrogative adverbs appear at the beginning of a question:

    Why did you break the cup?

- Adverbs can be made from adjectives:

    I am **serious** about going to bed early. ➡ Are you **seriously** going to bed early?

Adverbs

R ead the examples

walk **slowly**	eat **hurriedly**	dance **wildly**	he sings **well**
she **never** tells a lie	work **seriously**	speak **softly**	cough **loudly**
	he dances **gracefully**	she gazes **adoringly**	

A ttempt it yourself

Appropriate adverb

1. Use an appropriate adverb to finish the following sentences.

   (a) The tortoise walks _____.

   (b) The lion roared _____.

   (c) She beeped the horn _____.

   (d) He folded the blanket _____.

   (e) Ethan passed his test and skipped home _____.

   (f) I didn't mean to break the plate, I did it _____.

   (g) Jenny is waiting for her friend to finish an exam so she waits _____.

   (h) If I spent some time in France I could speak French _____.

   (i) John has only ten minutes before practice starts so he eats his dinner _____.

   (j) On the last day of term the teacher addressed the class _____.

M ore practice

Adjective transformation

2. Change these adjectives into adverbs.

   (a) wonderful ➜ _____
   (b) loud ➜ _____
   (c) sad ➜ _____
   (d) sweet ➜ _____
   (e) beautiful ➜ _____
   (f) brave ➜ _____
   (g) bad ➜ _____
   (h) selfish ➜ _____
   (i) anxious ➜ _____
   (j) gentle ➜ _____

Sentence glow-up

3. Use as many adjectives and adverbs as you can to enliven these sentences.

Example
Mary walked to the shop. → **Elegant old** Mary walked **jubilantly** to the **chic** flower shop.

(a) The dog ate his bone.

(b) Lucy finished her homework.

(c) Chloe ran to school.

(d) Luke hopped upstairs.

(e) The principal closed the school gates.

(f) The dinner is on the table.

(g) The shoe is in the hall.

(h) Ben fell off the trampoline.

(i) The windows were clean.

(j) The storm kept me up.

More practice

Adverb finder

4. Underline the adverbs in the following passage.

> Last Sunday Scott got a lift from his grandad to his friend Sam's birthday party. He ran quickly to his grandad's house after his football match. There was lots of traffic so his grandad had to drive slowly. 'Are we going to be late?' Scott asked worriedly. 'Please god we won't,' his grandad answered hopefully. 'I could get out and walk,' Scott replied enthusiastically. He carefully opened the car door and proceeded to run rapidly to Sam's house. He wasn't entirely sure which house was Sam's, so he took a guess, walked hesitantly up the path and rang the doorbell nervously. Sam answered and greeted Scott joyfully.

Another fact

Examine the following sentence.

> She made me laugh **wildly** and **loudly**.

Retrieval exercise

In your own words, write down what an adverb is. Include an example to help you revise.

An adverb is ....
....
....
....
....
An example of a adverb: ....

Louder than Words » Grammar Guide

PREPOSITIONS

Get to grips with ... prepositions

Prepositions are words that show the relationship between nouns or pronouns and other words in a sentence.

Preposition list

above	after	against	among	as	at
before	behind	below	beneath	beside	but
by	for	from	in	inside	into
like	near	of	on	onto	out
past	since	than	through	to	towards
under	unlike	until	up	with	within

Read the examples

The road leads **onto** the beach.

My dog sleeps **in** its bed **near** the fire.

Your keys are **on** the shelf **above** the couch.

Attempt it yourself

Phrasing prepositions

1. (a) Write your own sentences using these prepositions.

   (i) behind

   ....

   (ii) from

   ....

   (iii) near

   ....

   (iv) through

   ....

(v) since

....

(b) Finish these sentences by adding a preposition and an ending.

(i) Paige jumped _____.

(ii) Caiden sat _____.

(iii) The old man walked _____.

(iv) Amir is travelling _____.

(v) The vet looked _____.

More practice
Provide the prepositions

2. Underline the prepositions in the following excerpt from *The Witches* by Roald Dahl.

> We were in the big living-room of her house in Oslo and I was ready for bed. The curtains were never drawn in that house, and through the windows I could see huge snowflakes falling slowly on to an outside world that was as black as tar. My grandmother was tremendously old and wrinkled, with a massive wide body which was smothered in grey lace. She sat there majestic in her armchair, filling every inch of it. Not even a mouse could have squeezed in to sit beside her. I myself, just seven years old, was crouched on the floor at her feet, wearing pyjamas, dressing-gown and slippers.

More practice
Prepositions in prose

3. **(a)** Write the opening of a short story inspired by one of these images.

A.

B.

Louder than Words ▶▶ Grammar Guide

Short story title:
....
....
....
....
....
....
....
....
....
....
....
....
....
....

(b) Now underline all of the prepositions that you included in your short story opening.

Another fact

Examine the following sentence from *Autumn* by Ali Smith.

> Flatland **behind** the dunes. Trees **past** the flatland, a line **of** woods, all the way back round **to** the sea again.

Retrieval exercise

In your own words, write down what a preposition is. Include an example to help you revise.

A preposition is ....
....
....
....
....

An example of a preposition: ....

CONJUNCTIONS

Get to grips with ... conjunctions

Conjunctions are words that link phrases or other words together.

Some sentences are made up of more than one clause (a group of words that contains a subject and a verb that have a relationship). These clauses are often joined together using conjunctions to make more interesting sentences.

Conjunctions are like a bridge, linking two phrases together and helping sentences to flow better.

There are three main types of conjunctions:

- **Coordinating conjunctions:** These conjunctions connect two parts of a sentence.

  Examples
  and   but   yet   so   nor   or

- **Correlative conjunctions:** These conjunctions are in pairs and help in comparisons.

  Examples
  either ... or
  neither ... nor
  not only ... but also ...
  whether ... or ...

- **Subordinating conjunctions:** These conjunctions join the more important clause to the less important one.

  Examples
  while   since   because   although   unless

Read the examples

although	by	just	supposing	whereas
as	even if	nor	otherwise	whenever
as long as	despite	providing	until	whether
before	for	so	when	while

Louder than Words » Grammar Guide

Read the following passage.

> I tried on a new top. It was black. It was sparkly. It didn't really fit me. I thought it was the right size. The woman in the shop was really unhelpful. She offered assistance. 'You need a different size,' she said. She smirked.

Here is the same passage, this time improved by the use of conjunctions.

> I tried on a new top **that** was black **and** sparkly, **but** it didn't really fit me **even though** I thought it was the right size. The woman in the shop was really unhelpful, **despite** offering assistance. 'You need a different size,' she said **while** smirking.

📷 For the gram

You have probably learned that you should never start a sentence with a conjunction in formal writing, but you can use 'and' or 'but' at the start of a sentence if you are writing a story or an informal text.

Attempt it yourself

Conjunct it

1. In each case, use a conjunction to create one sentence.

   (a) Jane likes to eat chocolate. Jane eats it every day.

   ....
   ....

   (b) Martin listens to podcasts. Martin enjoys long walks.

   ....
   ....

   (c) She would have gone to the party but she couldn't. She didn't have a costume.

   ....
   ....

(d) He supports Man United. His brother supports Liverpool.

....
....
....

(e) They will continue to work at the restaurant. They don't get paid very well.

....
....
....

More practice

Create with conjunctions

2. Write three sentences using conjunctions from the examples given in the table on page 27.

....
....
....

Conjunction!

3. Come up with a conjunction for each letter in the word.

C onjunction!
O ....
N ....
J ....
U ....
N ....
C onjunction!
T ....
I ....
O ....
N ....

29

More practice

Conjunction finder

4. Underline the conjunctions in this blurb for the book *Word Nerd* by Susin Nielsen.

> A self-described 'friendless nerd,' he moves from place to place every couple of years with his overprotective mother, Irene. When some bullies at his new school almost kill him by slipping a peanut into his sandwich – even though they know he has a deathly allergy – Ambrose is philosophical. Irene, however, is not and decides that Ambrose will be home-schooled.

5. Write your own blurb for a book you have recently read. Try to include at least three conjunctions.

Conjunction detective

6. Open any page of your English textbook, novel or school journal. Make a list of all the conjunctions you can find on that page.

Because, because!

7. Write five sentences using 'because' as a conjunction.

....
....
....
....
....

Another fact

Here are some more examples of conjunctions.

| that | if | how | however | in case | in spite of |

Retrieval exercise

In your own words, write down what a conjunction is. Include examples to help you revise.

A conjunction is ....
....
....
....
....

Three examples of a coordinating conjunction: ....
....
....

Two examples of a correlative conjunction: ....
....
....

One example of a subordinating conjunction: ....
....

CAPITAL LETTERS

Get to grips with ... capital letters

A capital letter should be used when:
- starting a sentence
- using the personal pronoun 'I'
- writing days of the week, months of the year and holidays
- naming countries, languages, nationalities and religions
- naming people and titles
- naming companies and organisations
- naming places and monuments
- writing titles of books, poems and songs
- abbreviating.

Read the examples

Lithuania	Google	Mary
Saturday	Microsoft	BBC
CMO	Kildare	*The New Friday*
Jimmy	January	Taj Mahal
Dr O'Connor	Easter	'Rebecca's Afterthought'

Attempt it yourself

Add the capitals

1. Rewrite the following sentences using capital letters where appropriate.

   (a) john got a new bag for school.

   ....
   ....

   (b) During the cruise, the ship stopped in italy, spain and france.

   ....
   ....

(c) My aunt works tirelessly for focus ireland.

(d) When we go to Paris on the school trip, I want to visit the eiffel tower.

(e) 'You and i need to talk,' she said sternly after the class had ended.

(f) We did a survey last tuesday and 35 per cent of the class had birthdays in april.

(g) James, michael and luke were all absent today.

(h) I don't know what they do but all I know is that his father works for rté, and his mother works for the hse.

(i) Can you believe that sheila and i have been friends since primary school?

(j) *tokyo ghoul* is my favourite anime series.

Louder than Words ▶ Grammar Guide

More practice
CAPITAL LETTER

2. Come up with a word that takes a capital letter for each letter.

C anada
A
P
I
T
A
L

L
E
T
T
E
R

More practice
Capitals rule!

3. (a) Rewrite the following sentences using capital letters where appropriate.

(i) *harry potter and the philosopher's stone* is my favourite childhood book.

(ii) i play hockey on mondays, tuesdays and thursdays.

(iii) 'god, mr maloney is such a pain!' cried joanne.

(iv) he and i never really saw eye to eye.

(v) google and facebook have offices in dublin.

....
....

(vi) i would usually be in work but it's st patrick's day so we are taking friday off as well.

....
....

(vii) she is really impressive. she speaks four languages: italian, mandarin, spanish and english.

....
....

(b) Revise the rules for using capital letters below. Write the number of the rule being used against each of the sentences above. In some cases more than one rule might be in use.

Rules

A capital letter is used when:
1. starting a sentence
2. using the personal pronoun 'I'
3. writing days of the week, months of the year and holidays
4. naming countries, languages, nationalities and religions
5. naming people and titles
6. naming companies and organisations
7. naming places and monuments
8. writing titles of books, poems and songs
9. abbreviating.

Example

queen elizabeth II lives in buckingham palace. → Queen Elizabeth II lives in Buckingham Palace. → Rules 1, 5, 7

(c) Write five sentences demonstrating as many of the rules on page 35 as you can. Remember, a sentence can have more than one capital letter.

Another fact

Here are some more examples of capital letters in action.

Bailey	Pepsi Max	Hermione
Dairy Milk	Malahide Castle	USA

Retrieval exercise

In your own words, write down when a capital letter should be used. Include an example to help you revise.

Capital letters are used when

An example of a capital letter in action:

FULL STOPS

Get to grips with ... full stops

Full stops (.) show where a sentence ends. They indicate that a point has been made and that you are ready to move on to the next sentence.

Full stops are important because they help a reader understand your writing and break up sentences that would otherwise be too long and confusing.

Read the examples

He walked along the bay, taking in the stunning views. He couldn't believe his luck. He was finally here.

📷 For the gram

The easiest way to decide where to put a full stop is to read the text aloud and see where the natural breaks and pauses are. Remember that full stops are used to create full and clear sentences and to show that the sentence has ended. Without full stops in the above example, the sentence would be very long and rambling.

Attempt it yourself

Stop it!

1. Rewrite the following passage by inserting full stops where necessary. Remember that a capital letter is required at the start of a sentence.

   The housing crisis is one of the biggest issues in Ireland today supply is not meeting demand while rental costs are rising all the time there are people living on the streets in all our major cities these people do not have the appropriate supports in order to get them off the streets it seems that quite a large number of people are struggling with the cost of living this is the money required for rent, bills and food – the basic necessities in life

Louder than Words >> Grammar Guide

More practice

Stop and describe

2. Write 3–5 sentences on one of the following images, making sure to use full stops.

A.

B.

C.

More practice

Edit and correct

3. Rewrite the following sentences, adding and removing full stops and capital letters as necessary.

(a) jodie ran. aLl the Way home

(b) The fox was brown. furry and Cunning

(c) the rain fell. from the tree branchEs

(d) marta, billy and tom All. had soup fOr Lunch last Tuesday

(e) i've been all Over the World with my Band we are called the lost tribe wE PLAY jazz mostly

(f) the first Monday in October is always wet the sky is always Grey i never know What to Wear

(g) the Dog ran quickly To avoid getting His Lead. attached he loved walks but hated wearing it

(h) 'i can't find my ipad,' shouted lily 'i had it an Hour Ago'

(i) the jewish holiday of haunkkah is usually celebrated In December

....
....

A nother fact

Full stops are also used in abbreviations. Examine the use of full stops in these abbreviations.

I woke up at 7 **a.m**. on **Wed**. morning.   We have dinner every **Mon**. at **6 p.m.**

📷 For the gram

When **a.m.** or **p.m.** comes at the end of a sentence, you don't need to add another full stop.

Example
Even though school has finished for summer, I still get up every morning at **6 a.m..**   ✘
Even though school has finished for summer, I still get up every morning at **6 a.m.**   ✓

Also, full stops are not necessary in acronyms. You just need capital letters!

Examples
UK   UFO   WHO

R etrieval exercise

In your own words, write down when a full stop should be used. Include an example to help you revise.

Full stops are used to
....
....
....
....
....

An example of a full stop in action:

40

COMMAS

Get to grips with ... commas

A comma (,) is a punctuation mark used to:
- separate adjectives
- separate items in a list
- indicate a pause.

Read the examples

- Separating adjectives

  The sand was grainy, dry, warm, smooth and soft beneath my feet.

- Separating items in a list

  This summer I am planning to visit Donegal, Sligo, Mayo, Clare and Galway.

- Indicating a pause

  Ailbhe wasn't just nervous, she was petrified.

Attempt it yourself

Complete with commas

1. Correct the following sentences by marking where commas should be added to separate adjectives.

   (a) The long narrow road stretched out in front of my eyes.
   (b) We moved into our big new house in the summer.
   (c) I couldn't wait to hold the tiny cuddly cute baby.
   (d) This book is full of drama excitement suspense and tension.
   (e) My bedroom is big bright colourful comforting and warm.

2. Correct the following sentences by marking where commas should be added to separate the items in each list.

   (a) I'm packing sandwiches oranges rice-cakes jellies and juice for our picnic.
   (b) Don't forget to bring your tickets passport money and phone.
   (c) For this recipe you will need eggs sugar flour vanilla and almonds.
   (d) My hobbies include dance gymnastics camogie swimming painting piano and baking.
   (e) Students will need a calculator pencil pen geometry set ruler and rubber for their maths exam.

Louder than Words » Grammar Guide

3. Correct the following sentences by marking where commas should be added to indicate a pause.

  (a) Wait are you sure?

  (b) Let's go to the beach Harvey.

  (c) I'm not sure what do you think?

  (d) Molly you better be there when I get home.

  (e) Shona is as you can hear from her performance a talented singer.

More practice

Correct commas

4. (a) Indicate with a tick ✓ the sentences with the correct use of commas.

  (i) With a huge smile, he opened the present. ☐

  (ii) My dog is fluffy, cuddly and playful. ☐

  (iii) As the sun went down the sky turned a beautiful, orange. ☐

  (iv) My favourite colours are, yellow, blue and green. ☐

  (v) I bought my mum perfume, candles, flowers and chocolates. ☐

  (vi) The boy's face was freckly pale, cheeky and wild. ☐

  (vii) Until yesterday I didn't know, where you lived. ☐

  (viii) The woman laughed, coughed and choked in shock! ☐

(b) Now rewrite the incorrect sentences. Ensure commas are used in the correct places.

Commas

More practice

Custom commas

5. Write a description of the following images using adjectives separated by commas in the correct places.

(a)

(b)

(c)

(d)

43

Louder than Words >> Grammar Guide

Shop, shop, shop

6. Write the following shopping list as a sentence using commas.

Shopping list
- milk
- butter
- meat
- rice
- eggs
- juice
- bread
- fruits
- onion

Another fact

Examine the following excerpt from *Beautiful World, Where Are You* by Sally Rooney. The commas are used to indicate a pause.

> She glanced at the screen of her phone, on which was displayed a messaging interface, and then looked back at the door again. It was late March, the bar was quiet, and outside the window to her right the sun was beginning to set over the Atlantic.

Retrieval exercise

In your own words, write down when a comma should be used. Include examples to help you revise.

Commas are used to

An example of a comma in action:

(a) Separate adjectives:

(b) Separate items in a list:

(c) Indicate a pause:

QUESTION MARKS

Get to grips with ... question marks

A question mark (?) is used at the end of a sentence to show that it is a question rather than a statement.

Read the examples

What time is it?
Why are all the windows open?
When will we leave?
Where is the park?

'How come you took that route?' asked Delilah.
'Can we have sweets after dinner?' pleaded Noah.

Attempt it yourself

Mark the question mark

1. Rewrite the following sentences, inserting a question mark in the correct place. Make sure to insert full stops where necessary.

   (a) Why did she ask you to come

   ....
   ....

   (b) 'Where would we get the best value' queried the man

   ....
   ....

   (c) 'Should we ask them to come' wondered Sophia

   ....
   ....

   (d) Who is that man coming over the hill

   ....
   ....

Louder than Words » Grammar Guide

(e) 'Could we try a different restaurant' asked Henry

(f) 'Can we go down the slide again' the children pleaded

(g) 'How long is left in the match' the fan enquired

(h) When will this lesson be finished

More practice

Question Q&A

2. Write a potential question to the answers below. Remember to use question marks.

(a) Q:

A: There are ten.

(b) Q:

A: I'm going to go in the wintertime.

(c) Q:

A: I would if I had more followers

(d) Q:

A: Because I asked him to.

(e) Q:

A: Surely not!

(f) Q: ....

    A: Yeah, he got detention for it.

(g) Q: ....

    A: I wish!

(h) Q: ....

    A: No, he used to, but he lives in London now.

More practice

A question of crime

3. Read the following passage, which details information given to Gardaí by the witness of a crime. Write a list of eight questions that you think the Gardaí asked which resulted in this information.

> It was approximately 7 a.m. on Saturday morning. I was out walking the dog, which I usually do at about 7.30 a.m., but I was a little earlier that morning because I woke up earlier. I heard a loud smash. I noticed two men outside the front of the house. I didn't see their faces but one had black hair. The other one had his hood up. They were both dressed in dark clothes. The man with his hood up was reaching through the smashed window trying to open the door. The other man was using a crowbar trying to prise open the door. I realised then that they were breaking into the house. It was obvious there was nobody home as the alarm was going off and there was no car in the driveway. I let out a roar from across the road. The men ran. I saw them getting into a black car. I couldn't see the full number plate but it definitely started with 10 D.

Q.1: ....

Q.2: ....

Q.3: ....

Q.4: ....

Q.5: ....

Q.6: ....

Q.7: ....

Q.8: ....

Louder than Words >> Grammar Guide

Ask about it

4. Write a list of questions that would you like to ask about the two images below.

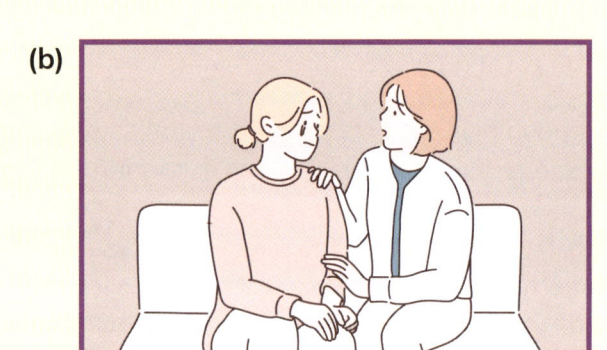

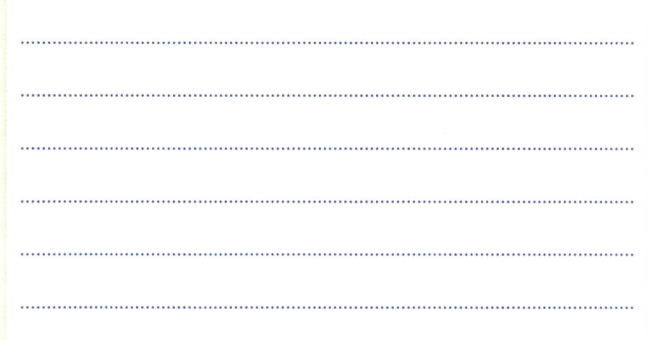

(a)

(b)

Another fact

Examine the following sentence.

'What are we having for dinner**?**' enquired Mark.

Retrieval exercise

In your own words, write down when a question mark should be used. Include an example to help you revise.

Question marks are used to

An example of a question mark in action:

EXCLAMATION MARKS

Get to grips with ... exclamation marks

To 'exclaim' is to cry out or express a strong feeling. An exclamation mark (!) is used at the end of a sentence to show when something is surprising, exciting or frustrating.

Usually, exclamation marks show:

- strong feelings
- urgent instructions or orders
- interjections, such as 'Oh! I understand'.

Remember that exclamation marks take the place of a full stop.

Read the examples

| I don't believe it! | Don't you dare! | Surprise! |
| I am so excited! | Yay! Our team won! | Please help me! |

Attempt it yourself

Add the exclamation marks

1. Insert an exclamation mark in the correct place in the following sentences.

    (a) Don't argue with me
    (b) Warning
    (c) Stop being so annoying
    (d) Mum Harry's pinching me.
    (e) This is the best present ever
    (f) Caution Falling rocks.
    (g) Look out
    (h) Sit down now
    (i) I am warning you
    (j) Yes We won the match.

More practice

Everybody exclaim

2. Sort the following sentences by writing them into the correct category in the table on page 50.

    (a) Ouch! That really hurts!
    (b) I am sick and tired of your bad behaviour!
    (c) Make your way to the exit immediately!
    (d) Don't come near me ever again!
    (e) Yes! Our school came first in the debating league!
    (f) I hate you!
    (g) Break is over. Go to class!
    (h) Enough! That's the end of the game.
    (i) Go straight to the principal's office!
    (j) I can't believe I made the final!

Louder than Words » Grammar Guide

Strong feeling	Urgent instruction or order	Interjection

More practice
Exclamation marks in expression

3. Write a phrase that includes an exclamation mark inspired by each of these feelings.

   (a) Shock:

   (b) Excitement:

   (c) Anger:

4. Write a short paragraph inspired by each of the images, including at least one exclamation mark in each paragraph.

   (a)

(b)

(c)

Another fact

Examine the following sentence from *The Perks of Being a Wallflower* by Stephen Chbosky.

CHARLIE! SHUT UP! OKAY?! JUST SHUT UP!

Retrieval exercise

In your own words, write down when an exclamation mark should be used. Include an example to help you revise.

Exclamation marks are used to

An example of an exclamation mark in action:

APOSTROPHES

Get to grips with ... apostrophes

An apostrophe (') is a punctuation mark used to indicate possession or the omission of letters.

Indicating possession:

- When using an apostrophe to show that something belongs to someone, you should place the apostrophe before the 's'.
- When using an apostrophe to show that something belongs to more than one person, you should place the apostrophe after the 's'.
- Some plural words, such as 'children', 'sheep' and 'feet', do not end in 's'. In this case, you should add an apostrophe and an 's' after the word to indicate ownership.

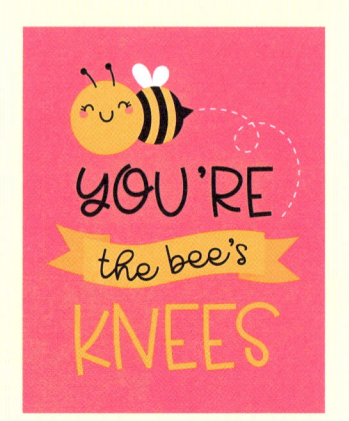

Indicating missing letters:

Sometimes certain words are run together to form one word, meaning letters are left out. These words are known as **contractions**. ('Contraction' means 'becoming smaller'.)

Example
Don't forget to check your grammar and spelling!

The word 'don't' is a contraction of 'do not'. The writer runs the two words together by dropping the letter 'o' in 'not' and replacing it with an apostrophe.

Read the examples

- Possession or belonging

Singular	Plural
The boy's bag	The twins' outfits
Mary's coat	The teachers' union
The man's watch	The children's playground

- Contractions

I will → I'll	would not → wouldn't
You are → You're	She will not → She won't
We are → We're	You cannot → You can't
could not → couldn't	I am → I'm

Apostrophes

📷 For the gram

Remember that **it's** is a contraction of **it is**. In this case, the apostrophe does not indicate possession. **Its** (without an apostrophe) is used to show possession or belonging.

Examples
It's going to rain. → **It is** going to rain.
The dog ate **its** food. → The dog ate the food **belonging to it**.

A ttempt it yourself

It's right, it's wrong

1. Indicate whether the use of apostrophes in the following sentences are correct ✓ or incorrect ✗.

   (a) In school we all use iPad's.
   (b) It's a good idea to drink plenty of water.
   (c) Here are one persons' study tips.
   (d) Your pet can be your saviour! Take care of it's needs.
   (e) Janet's going to meet us there.
   (f) Paul's collection of poems will be published this summer.
   (g) It's difficult for me to understand poems that were written before my time.
   (h) The correct use of apostrophe's is a mystery to me.
   (i) The sun was magnificent, it's rays were sparkling on the waves.
   (j) Five students' poems will be printed in the next newsletter.

M ore practice

It's A, it's B

2. Indicate with a tick ✓ the sentence with the correct use of apostrophes in the following pairs.

(a)	A. Where are the children's jackets?	B. Where are the childrens' jackets?
(b)	A. When you wake up in the morning, don't stay in your pyjamas.	B. When you wake up in the morning, do'nt stay in your pyjamas.
(c)	A. It's not fair that we can't go to the party.	B. Its not fair that we can't go to the party.
(d)	A. Shanes' tent was wrecked after the trip.	B. Shane's tent was wrecked after the trip.

53

Louder than Words >> Grammar Guide

(e)	A. Lets' go over to Jame's house. ☐	B. Let's go over to James's house. ☐
(f)	A. If you weren't keeping yourself busy, you'd go crazy! ☐	B. If you wer'ent keeping yourself busy, yo'ud go crazy! ☐
(g)	A. Sam's books were left on the shelf with the other pupils' books. ☐	B. Sam's books were left on the shelf with the other pupils's books. ☐
(h)	A. I know I'll enjoy my summer holidays once my exams are over. ☐	B. I know Il'l enjoy my summer holidays once my exams are over. ☐
(i)	A. Set small goals every day. Student's should set study target's. Its a good way to keep your mind active. ☐	B. Set small goals every day. Students should set study targets. It's a good way to keep your mind active. ☐
(j)	A. Lets all do what we can to stay safe, healthy and happy. ☐	B. Let's all do what we can to stay safe, healthy and happy. ☐

More practice

Add the apostrophes

3. Indicate where apostrophes should be inserted in the following excerpt from *Noughts & Crosses* by Malorie Blackman.

> 'Honestly, Mrs Hadley,' said Meggie McGregor, wiping her eyes. 'That sense of humour of yours will be the death of me yet!'
>
> Jasmine Hadley allowed herself a rare giggle. 'The things I tell you Meggie. Its lucky were such good friends!'
>
> Meggies smile wavered only slightly. She looked out across the vast lawn at Callum and Sephy. Her son and her employers daughter. They were good friends playing together. *Real* good friends. No barriers. No boundaries. Not yet anyway. It was a typical early summers day, light and bright and, in the Hadley household anyway, not a cloud in their sky.
>
> 'Excuse me, Mrs Hadley,' Sarah Pike, Mrs Hadleys secretary, approached from the house. She had shoulder-length straw-coloured hair and timid green eyes which appeared permanently startled. 'Im sorry to disturb you but your husband has just arrived. Hes in the study.'

4. Tick ✓ the correct statement to show that you know when you should use an apostrophe.

Use an apostrophe to ...	
Indicate belonging and show abbreviations	☐
Indicate belonging and show where letters are missing	☐
Indicate belonging and show where letters are added	☐

Apostrophes

Another fact

- Do not use an apostrophe in plural nouns.

  Examples
  The boy's **eye's** are green. ✗
  The **film's** in the upcoming festival are great. ✗

- If a word ends in an 's', you still add 's after it to indicate possession.

  Example
  The princes**s's** crown ✓

- Be careful not to mix up the following.

Possessive	Contraction
Its The dog licked its fur.	It's It's a nice day today. (It is …)
Theirs Our team was victorious over theirs in the quiz.	There's There's a good chance it will rain today. (There is …)
Your Your dress is nice.	You're You're late again. (You are …)
Whose Whose coats are these?	Who's Who's going to the party? (Who is going …?)

Retrieval exercise

In your own words, write down when an apostrophe should be used. Include examples to help you revise.

Apostrophes are used to
....
....
....
....
....

An example of an apostrophe in action:
(a) Possessive:
....
(b) Contraction:
....

Louder than Words >> Grammar Guide

QUOTATION MARKS

Get to grips with ... quotation marks

Quotation marks ('/') are used when writing direct speech or quoting what someone has said.

Example
'I love chocolate,' Laura admitted.

Punctuation, such as commas, full stops, question marks and exclamation marks, should be included within the closing quotation mark.

Example
'Can we please go there next year?' Hugo pleaded.

If a quote is a full sentence, it begins with a capital letter and the full stop is placed within the closing quotation mark.

Example
Seamus Heaney once said, 'I'm very conscious that people dear to me are alive in my imagination – poets in particular.'

If the quote is an incomplete sentence, the full stop is placed outside the closing quotation mark.

Example
In the poem 'Mid-Term Break', Heaney poignantly writes that his brother was in a 'four-foot box'.

📷 For the gram

If a quote begins with a capital letter, this is a useful indicator of when to put the full stop inside the quotation mark. However, be aware that proper nouns are capitalised, so don't necessarily indicate the start of a sentence.

Read the examples

'Have you had enough to eat?' asked Danni.
Mr Smith said we shouldn't be nervous because it was 'only a test'.
'I want another go!' Ava screamed.

Quotation marks

Attempt it yourself
Correct the quotation marks

1. Use a tick ✓ or an ✗ to indicate whether quotation marks have been used correctly in the following sentences.

    (a) 'She's coming, she's coming, yelled Annabelle.' ☐

    (b) The poet creates an upbeat tone when he writes 'summer celebrations'. ☐

    (c) Mr Lynch told us 'not to write in a red pen.' ☐

    (d) 'I'll be down in a minute!' called Lucy. ☐

    (e) 'Can we go swimming on Saturday'? Ben asked. ☐

    (f) 'I don't have the right book,' said Jess. ☐

    (g) 'Whoever gets there first has to save the table,' James instructed. ☐

    (h) 'Will we ask Olivia if she wants one too?' asked Mark. ☐

More practice
Make your choice

2. Indicate with a tick ✓ the sentence with the correct use of quotation marks in the following groups.

    (a) (i)   Emma said, 'I really hate when it rains'. ☐

      (ii)   'Emma said,' I really hate when it rains. ☐

      (iii) Emma 'said, I really hate when it rains.' ☐

      (iv) Emma said, 'I really hate when it rains.' ☐

    (b) (i)   'We won the match! Jamie roared.' ☐

      (ii)   'We won the match!' Jamie roared. ☐

      (iii) 'We won the match! Jamie' roared. ☐

      (iv) We won the match! 'Jamie roared'. ☐

    (c) (i)   'Let's go' to the beach, Amber suggested. ☐

      (ii)   'Let's go to the beach, Amber suggested.' ☐

      (iii) 'Let's go to the beach, Amber' suggested. ☐

      (iv) 'Let's go to the beach,' Amber suggested. ☐

    (d) (i)   'Could we try again? Alex asked'. ☐

      (ii)   Could we try again? 'Alex asked'. ☐

      (iii) 'Could we try again'? Alex asked. ☐

      (iv) 'Could we try again?' Alex asked. ☐

Louder than Words » Grammar Guide

More practice

Quotation mark rewrite

3. Rewrite the following quotes using quotation marks.

   (a) Hi Molly, how was the match?

   (b) We could aim to get a coffee before the shops close.

   (c) Fine! You can come too, said her brother angrily.

   (d) Maya Angelou once said that people will never forget how you made them feel.

   (e) Can we get some ice-cream?

   (f) I don't think you should be doing that, Mrs Wilson commented.

   (g) I cannot wait until the exams are over!

   (h) Come on, hurry up! said Sarah, holding the door open.

Quotation marks

Quote the conversation

4. Write the conversation that you imagine the two characters are having in the images below. Use quotation marks, adverbs and adjectives to create a really descriptive piece of writing, e.g. 'You have got to be kidding', said Holly excitedly.

(a) ....

(b) ....

Another fact

Examine the following sentence.

The magazine said, 'Country music will be the next biggest genre in the industry.'

Retrieval exercise

In your own words, write down when quotation marks should be used. Include examples to help you revise.

Quotation marks are used to ....

An example of quotation marks in action: ....

SYNONYMS

Get to grips with ... synonyms

A synonym is a word or phrase that means the same thing as another word or phrase. It is an alternative that you can use to vary your vocabulary and prevent your writing from being repetitive and boring.

Synonyms can be found in a **thesaurus**. While a dictionary lists words and their definitions, a thesaurus lists words and their synonyms. A thesaurus allows you to search for a word to find a list of alternative words meaning the same thing.

Read the examples

tiny is a synonym for small
delighted is a synonym for happy
furious is a synonym for angry
received is a synonym for got
terrible is a synonym for bad
kid is a synonym for child

boring   tedious

Attempt it yourself

Synonym pairs

1. Match the words with their synonyms.

hate	cheerful
fast	dull
cry	brilliant
interesting	adore
speak	detest
good	wail
happy	quick
boring	freezing
cold	talk
love	intriguing

More practice

Synonym tick

2. Indicate with a tick ✓ the synonyms for the following words.

   (a) ill
   - dull ☐
   - sick ☐
   - slow ☐

   (b) tired
   - exhausted ☐
   - sore ☐
   - giant ☐

   (c) jump
   - transfer ☐
   - transmit ☐
   - hop ☐

   (d) replied
   - phoned ☐
   - answered ☐
   - atc ☐

   (e) tasty
   - full ☐
   - delicious ☐
   - burnt ☐

   (f) lovely
   - appealing ☐
   - astonished ☐
   - entertaining ☐

   (g) splendid
   - glitter ☐
   - musical ☐
   - fantastic ☐

   (h) always
   - sometimes ☐
   - never ☐
   - forever ☐

More practice

Select a synonym

3. Rewrite the following sentences by replacing the underlined words with synonyms.

   Example
   Mary ate the apple quickly. → Mary *munched* the apple *rapidly*.

   (a) Joe went to the shop.

   ....

   (b) Adam is a good student.

   ....

   (c) Sophie is very kind.

   ....

Louder than Words ›› Grammar Guide

(d) Brian is <u>happy</u> he won.

....

(e) Emma is <u>angry</u> at the situation.

....

(f) We were all <u>entertained</u> by the stories.

....

(g) I think we should <u>go</u>.

....

(h) I am <u>glad</u> you are feeling <u>better</u>.

....

(i) The car is parked <u>near</u> to the road.

....

Another fact

Examine the following statement.

Depict and **portray** are both synonyms for **show**.

Retrieval exercise

In your own words, write down what a synonym is. Include an example to help you revise.

A synonym is ....

....

....

....

....

An example of a word and its synonym: ....

ANTONYMS

Get to grips with ... antonyms

An antonym is a word that is opposite in meaning to another.

Read the examples

small is an antonym for large	better is an antonym for worse
disappointed is an antonym for delighted	fast is an antonym for slow
happy is an antonym for furious	bore is an antonym for amuse

Attempt it yourself

Antonyms pairs

1. Match the words with their antonyms.

conflict
cheap
rare
fierce
heavy
soft
hard-working
capture
break
numerous

mild
few
lazy
fix
peace
release
light
expensive
common
hard

More practice

Antonym tick

2. Indicate with a tick ✓ the antonyms for the following words.

(a) whisper
   hush ☐   shout ☐   cry ☐

(b) tight
   loose ☐   squeezed ☐   full ☐

(c) furious
   heated ☐   feverish ☐   calm ☐

(d) arrive
  check in ☐ depart ☐ tolerate ☐
(e) black
  screen ☐ white ☐ table ☐
(f) below
  deck ☐ roof ☐ above ☐
(g) birth
  death ☐ day ☐ name ☐
(h) best
  friend ☐ gift ☐ worst ☐

More practice

Opposites attract

3. Underline the antonyms in the following poem.

> He is big and she is small
> They are tiny and we are tall
> Lily is silent and Peter is loud
> Grace is shy whereas James is proud
> Sue is good and Jack is bad
> Ernie is happy but Ralph is sad
> I stay up all day while you are up all night
> Neither are wrong so both are right.

Another fact

Examine the following statement.

> **Hate** and **detest** are both antonyms for **love**.

Retrieval exercise

In your own words, write down what an antonym is. Include an example to help you revise.

An antonym is ....
....
....
....
An example of a word and its antonym: ....

SUPERLATIVES

Get to grips with ... superlatives

Superlatives are used to compare and show that something is the most or the greatest.

Identifying superlatives

- Describing something as *the most*
- Words ending in -est
- Words ending in -iest

Read the examples

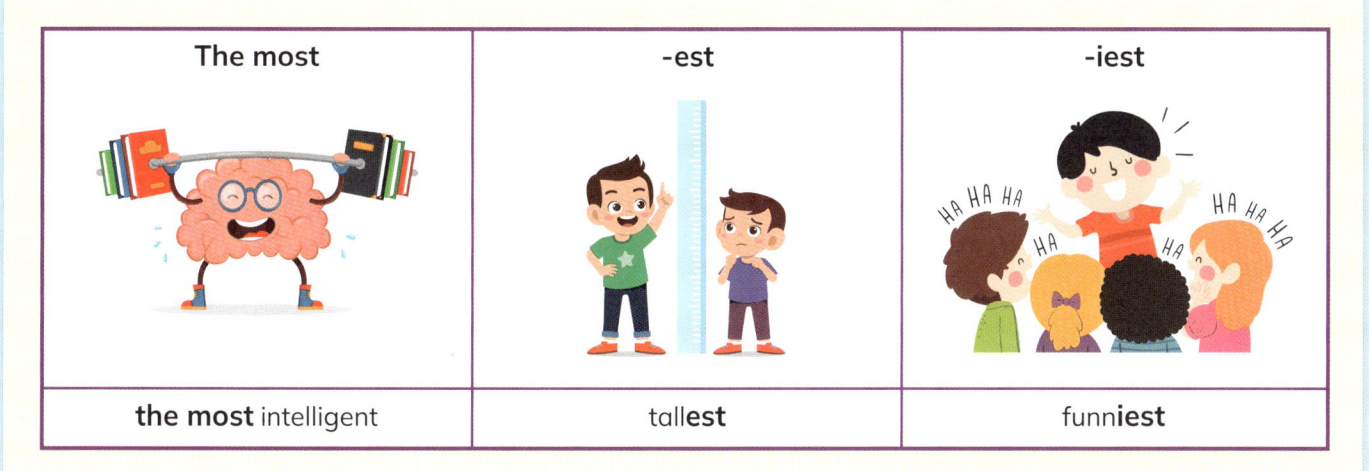

The most	-est	-iest
the most intelligent	tall**est**	funn**iest**

Attempt it yourself

Superlative sorting

1. Sort the underlined superlatives by writing them into the correct category in the table on page 66.

    (a) The <u>most exciting</u> time of my life was when I travelled to Africa.

    (b) Angie is the <u>happiest</u> baby.

    (c) The <u>biggest</u> present was from my nana.

    (d) That was the <u>longest</u> day ever!

    (e) I left the <u>most difficult</u> question until last.

    (f) I completed the <u>easiest</u> question first.

    (g) Strawberry is the <u>nicest</u> flavour.

    (h) The <u>most frustrating</u> thing about school is homework!

    (i) I needed help carrying the <u>heaviest</u> box.

    (j) My sister is the <u>most understanding</u> person in the world.

Louder than Words >> Grammar Guide

The most	-est	-iest

More practice

Superlative sentences

2. Write a sentence containing a superlative inspired by each of the images. Remember that your superlative should contain 'the most', '-est' or '-iest'.

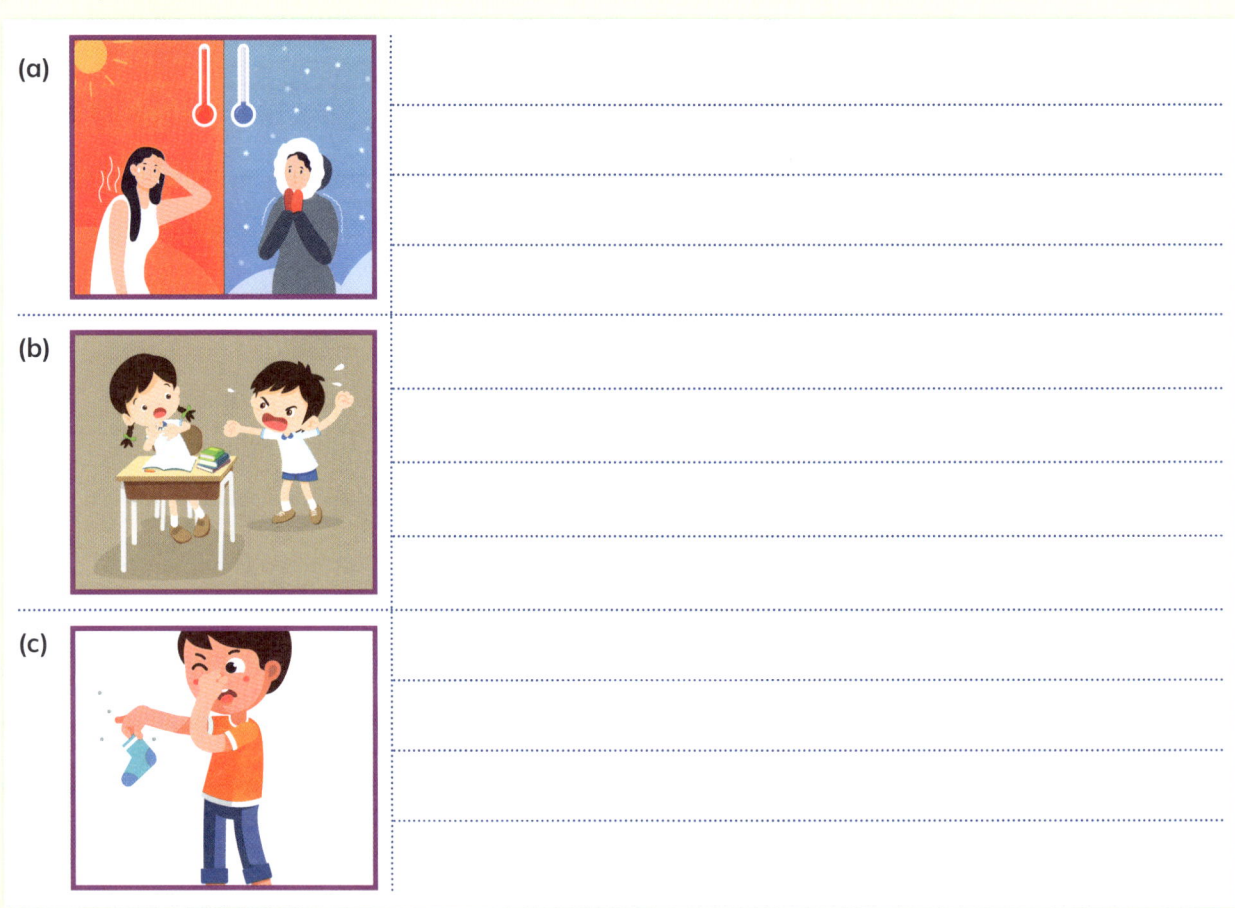

(a)

(b)

(c)

More practice

Seeing superlatives

3. Circle the superlatives.

| friendliest | tree | strangest | most famous | book |
| richest | most | interesting | smallest | the | highest |

4. Underline the superlatives in the following excerpt from *The Anthologist* by Nicholson Baker.

> It is turning out to be the most beautiful, most quiet, largest, most generous, sky-vaulted summer I've ever seen or known – inordinately blue, with greener leaves and taller trees than I can remember, and the sound of the lawnmowers all over this valley is a sound I could hum to forever.

5. Circle the correct superlative in the following sentences and write the correct sentence in the space provided.

   (a) On sports day, I ran the **fastiest / fastest** and won the race.

   ....

   (b) Ronaldo is the **greatest / most greatest** footballer.

   ....

   (c) Christopher wears the **colourfulest / most colourful** shorts.

   ....

   (d) Declan cut the **thickest / thickiest** slice of bread.

   ....

   (e) That was the **easiest / most easiest** test.

   ....

A nother fact

Examine the following sentence.

The **youngest** person in my family is my sister, Becky. She is also the **funniest** person with **the most hilarious** sense of humour.

R etrieval exercise

In your own words, write down what a superlative is. Include an example to help you revise.

A superlative is ....

....

....

An example of a superlative: ....

Louder than Words >> Grammar Guide

HOMOPHONES

Get to grips with ... homophones

A homophone is two or more words that sound the same but have different meanings. These words are often confused but can be avoided if you read back over your work carefully.

Read the examples

Were	Where	Wear	We're
Past tense of 'to be'	Meaning 'In what place?'	Verb meaning 'to have something, e.g. clothes, on'	A contraction: We are

To	Too	Two
Preposition meaning 'in the direction of'	Adverb meaning 'also' or 'excessively'	The number 2

Their	There	They're
Possessive adjective	Indicating a statement or the placement of an object	A contraction: They are

Your	You're
Possessive adjective	A contraction: You are

Our	Are
Possessive pronoun	Plural and second person singular of 'to be'

Except	Accept
Meaning 'not including', 'other than'	Meaning 'to undertake or consent to receive'

Effect	Affect
A noun meaning 'a change as a result of an action or cause'	A verb meaning 'to produce an effect'

Pain	Pane
Soreness or suffering from illness or injury	A sheet of glass, e.g 'windowpane'

Dye	Die
A noun meaning 'artificial colour for hair or clothes'	A verb meaning 'to stop living'

Homophones

Attempt it yourself

Which witch?

1. Identify the homophones represented by the images.

(a)

(b)

(c)

(d)

(e)

Louder than Words >> Grammar Guide

More practice

Homophone finder

2. Circle the correct homophone in the following sentences.

   (a) The students placed **there / their** books on the table and waited for the teacher to start the class.

   (b) What time is **you're / your** swimming lesson?

   (c) **Two / too** frogs jumped out of the murky lake.

   (d) Can you all **hear / here** me clearly?

   (e) If it was a nice day, I **wood / would** go outside to play.

   (f) You can slow the car down by pressing on the **break / brake**.

   (g) In autumn the trees are **bare / bear**.

   (h) The teacher writes the homework on the **board / bored** each day.

More practice

Homophone reminder

3. Circle the correct homophone in the following sentences.

   (a) We are not **allowed / aloud** to run in the corridor.

   (b) Her mum **knew / new** something was wrong.

   (c) I love chocolate-flavoured **serial / cereal** for breakfast.

   (d) I would love to **except / accept** your invitation.

   (e) I find it easier to study when it is **quite / quiet**.

   (f) **Our / Are** school holidays begin in June.

   (g) Dad had to **alter / altar** my costume before the performance.

   (h) The couple stood at the end of the **pier / peer** and watched the sunrise.

Homophones

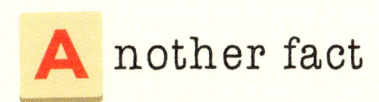

Another fact

Examine these homophones.

stationary	stationery
proceed	precede
allowed	aloud
complement	compliment
lose	loose

Verb	Noun
license	licence
practise	practice
affect	effect

Choose three homophones from the tables above and write a sentence for each, showing that you understand them.

....
....
....
....
....
....

Retrieval exercise

In your own words, write down what a homophone is. Include an example to help you revise.

A homophone is ....
....
....
....
....

An example of a homophone:

COMMON CLANGERS

Me and I

- Use the pronoun 'I' when the person speaking is doing the action, either alone or with someone else, e.g. 'Seán and I went to the match.'
- Use the pronoun 'me' when the person speaking is receiving the action of the verb in some way, either directly or indirectly, e.g. 'Simon went to the match with Seán and me.'

For the gram

If you want to check whether you should use 'I' or 'me', try saying the sentence without the other person to see if it makes sense.

Examples

'me went to the match' ✗   'Simon went to the match with I.' ✗

Fewer and less

- 'Fewer' means 'not as many'. Use 'fewer' to refer to countable nouns.
- 'Less' means 'not as much'. Use 'less' to refer to uncountable nouns.

Example
There were fewer cookies and less milk after Santa Claus had visited.

Formerly and formally

- The adverb 'formerly' means 'previously', 'in the past', 'at an earlier (former) time'.
- The adverb 'formally' means 'in a formal way' or 'following accepted forms, customs or conventions'.

Good and well

- 'Good' is an adjective, e.g. 'He is such a good little boy.'
- 'Well' is an adverb, e.g. 'I always work well under pressure.'

Literally and figuratively

- 'Literally' describes something that has actually happened, e.g. 'The driver took it literally when he was asked to drive straight through the roundabout.'
- 'Figuratively' describes something that has metaphorically happened, e.g. 'I was so embarrassed, I could have died.'

Specific and Pacific

- 'Specific' is an adjective meaning 'clearly defined or identified'.
- 'Pacific' is the ocean!

Can and may

- 'Can' is an auxiliary verb that is used to express mental and physical capability.
- 'May' is an auxiliary verb that is used to express permission.

Being and been

- 'Being' refers to the present or a continuous action.
- 'Been' refers to the past or to something that started in the past but is continuing into the present.

Now, show you understand the difference by writing a sentence for each word.

- me: ....

- I: ....

- fewer: ....

- less: ....

- formerly: ....

Louder than Words >> Grammar Guide

- formally: ....

- good: ....

- well: ....

- literally: ....

- figuratively: ....

- specific: ....

- Pacific: ....

- can: ....

- may: ....

- being: ....

- been: ....

GRAMMAR AT A GLANCE

Grammar point	Explanation	Examples
Adjective	Adjectives are words that are used to describe nouns or pronouns.	Dave painted the walls **white** and then washed the **dirty** brushes.
Adverb	Adverbs are used to describe verbs in more detail.	She snored **loudly**. He plays the violin **beautifully**. I **finally** finished, and I **never** want to do that again.
Antonym	An antonym is a word that is opposite in meaning to another.	bad and good full and empty
Apostrophe '	An apostrophe is a punctuation mark that is used to • indicate belonging • replace a missing letter.	The girl's face lit up. The men's team lost. I'll go to the shop.
Capital letter	A capital letter should be used when: • starting a sentence • using the personal pronoun 'I' • writing days of the week, months of the year and holidays • naming countries, languages, nationalities and religions • naming people and titles • naming companies and organisations • naming places and monuments • writing titles of books, poems and songs • abbreviating.	**O**n **M**onday, **J**amie and **I** spoke to the **F**rench teacher **M**r **L**yons about the project we were doing on the **TGV** in **F**rance.
Comma ,	A comma is a punctuation mark that is used to • separate adjectives • separate a list • indicate a pause.	She has long**,** wavy**,** blonde hair. We had coffee**,** tea and cakes. Darragh did not just leave the room**,** he ran out of the room.
Conjunction	Conjunctions are words that link phrases or other words together.	He will go with you **if** you ask him. I am very hungry, **but** the fridge is empty. **Although** it rains so much, we should still conserve water.

Louder than Words >> Grammar Guide

Grammar point	Explanation	Examples
Exclamation mark !	An exclamation mark is used at the end of a sentence to show when something is surprising, exciting or frustrating. Usually, exclamation marks show: - strong feelings - urgent instruction or orders - interjections such as 'Oh! I understand'. Remember that exclamation marks take the place of a full stop.	Don't you dare! Damn! I stubbed my toe! Everyone, inside now!
Full stop .	Full stops show where a sentence ends.	I ran down the stairs. My coat was hanging on the banister. I grabbed it and ran.
Homophone	Homophones are words that sound the same but have different spellings and meanings.	leak/leek pause/paws die/dye
Noun	A noun is a person, animal, place or thing.	Samir cow Brussels fence
Preposition	Prepositions are words that show the relationship between nouns or pronouns and other words in a sentence.	The road leads **onto** the beach. My dog sleeps **in** his bed near the fire.
Pronoun	Pronouns are words that are used instead of nouns.	**She** rescued the dog. **My** feet hurt.
Question mark ?	A question mark is used at the end of a statement to show that it is a question.	Could we watch something else?
Quotation marks '/'	Quotation marks should be used when - writing direct speech - quoting.	'I'm fine,' Annie replied, 'and how are you?' Heaney tells us that he saw his brother in 'a four-foot box.'
Superlative	Superlatives are used to compare and show that something is the most or the greatest.	the **most** intelligent the tall**est** the funn**iest**
Synonym	A synonym is a word or phrase that means the same thing as another word or phrase.	large/massive/gigantic/enormous
Tense	The meaning of a verb can be changed by changing the tense. The tense shows whether the action is taking place in the past, present or future.	I swam yesterday. I am swimming today. I will swim tomorrow.
Verb	Verbs are action (or doing) words. They are used to describe an action, state or occurrence. Every sentence needs a verb.	Méabh **smelled** the flowers. The mouse **ate** the cheese. Jacks **plays** the drums.